SELL
BUILD
GROW
FAST

ROADMAP TO DO 3X MORE PROJECTS
WITHOUT INVESTING MORE TIME, MONEY & ENERGY

SELL BUILD GROW FAST

DOUBLE YOUR SALES VELOCITY AT 9% OR MORE PREMIUM IN LESS THAN 30 DAYS

Ankur Hora

Worldwide Published by
Pendown Press

PENDOWN PRESS LLP

An ISO 9001 & ISO 14001 Certified Co.,

Regd. Office: 3767A, Kanhaiya Nagar,

Tri Nagar, Delhi-110035

Ph.: 8130886000, 9650072927, 8595249536

E-mail: info@pendownpress.com

Branch Office: 1A/2A, 20, Hari Sadan, Ansari Road,

Daryaganj, New Delhi-110002

Ph.: 011-45794768

Website: PendownPress.com

First Edition: 2024

Price: ₹699/-

ISBN: 978-93-5554-789-7

Layout and Cover Designed by Pendown Graphics Team
Printed and Bound in India by Thomson Press India Ltd.

Roadmap to Do 3X
More Projects Without
Investing More
Time, Money and Energy

Double Your Sales
Velocity at 9% Or More
Premium in
Less Than 30 Days

Dedication

This book is dedicated to growth-hungry real estate developers who aspire to become a "marketing-dominated sales-driven organization," aka the "purple cow" of their market.

May you unleash the best marketer in you and achieve your ambitions faster by reading sip sip kar ke (sip by sip) every page of this book!!

With gratitude, I dedicate the book to every developer who has helped me in this journey and certainly to my mentors, parents, my wife Aastha, and my kids, who have been a constant source of encouragement.

CONTENTS

Preface

After Working with real estate developers for over 18 Years, I have come to understand that there is a huge stake involved, and one right move can make or break it.

Thus, like playing chess when you are nearing checkmate, every move is critical. Similarly, in the real estate industry, every decision either costs you or adds millions to your pocket.

One common thread that remains consistent among you and more than 25,000 developers pan India is the desire to achieve ambitions faster. You want to start projects quickly, complete them, and exit swiftly, and then either parallelly undertake more projects or pursue additional projects every 5 or 10 years.

This book understands your deep desires and is curated to guide you directly on the path to achieving ambitions faster (without worrying about managing cash flow or increasing interest costs due to slower sales velocity).

This book will help you to identify your current situation and your desired situation in the context of sales velocity. It will assist you to understand the possible solutions you are currently using and why they may not be yielding the desired results. It delves into the root causes of why your conversions at every level, from enquiry to qualified enquiry, qualified enquiry to site visit, and site visit to paying customer, may not be meeting your expectations.

It will make you understand a very different approach to solve all your challenges related to sales. You will feel a noticeable difference in your conversion ratio and your team's conversion ratio. Then, you often wonder how you can train your team and hire consultants to train them, but these efforts also don't work permanently. You will understand the root cause of this issue, as you are addressing symptoms rather than the underlying cause.

This book will demystify that advertisement is not marketing, and it will show how your crores spent on advertisement can be saved simply by using the right marketing strategies.

In short, your sales velocity is less because your organization lacks a sequential psychological selling system which is followed by effective marketing that provides predictable sales using the same structure each and every time without any dependencies.

Let's discover and explore this new approach and create possibilities around it....

Foreword

People Buy Results... So Would You!

We carry a 100 years of real estate cumulative experience; however, we were not marketing it well.

Ankur was the first person who made me realize my life's mission: that I am not in the business of real estate but in the business of building happy communities by simplifying home buying science.

The unique marketing approach made me so approachable to my customers that I got to know about their secret desires and pain points, which served as real gunpowder to make bullets to win the hearts of prospects.

My ads' return on ad spend (ROAS) has started increasing, and referrals at zero cost have started increasing in just nine days of his mentoring.

The biggest victory is that, seeing the whole framework Ankur has implemented, I can sell the entire project of 1600 apartments by December 2024 instead of December 2025... exact one year earlier.

In no words can I thank or give back what Ankur has done for me!!!

Yashaswi Shroff
Home Buying Scientist, Marketing Director,
Alcove Realty, Kolkata

Foreword

I had a challenge of converting less than 1% of our enquiries into final paying customers.

I had tried every top course, mentor, or consultant. After meeting Ankur Bhai, he helped me to understand the root cause of that challenge.

I had a big question in my mind; whether I would be able to implement the science and if it would be worth investing my time on it!

Today, I can say that I, along with my sales team, have learned the science and used it. Our conversions have increased by 4x in less than 40 days.

I am grateful that I met Ankur Ji today.

Pratik Garg
Director, Tulsa Group, Siliguri

Foreword

Executive Committee Member at the National CREDAI Youth Wing referred Ankur to me with the assurance that he is a value bomb.

He is the Chanakya of real estate marketing, and the value he can bring to the table for any developer with his infectious energy is incomparable.

When I met Ankur, I understood that this guy understands the pulse of the builder and has close to two decades of experience. He knows the science and can increase the sales of any builder in less than a couple of weeks!

The approach he gave was based on such simple fundamentals, which 97% or more developers tend to ignore.

Listening to his wisdom, I recommended him to speak at the CREDAI YouthCon Conclave, and he was humble enough to accept the invitation.

Looking forward,

Dr. Adv. Harshul Salva
Director | M Realty, Mumbai | PHD | Author of 18 Books

Treating this book as just another read would be unjust. It's akin to underestimating the power of a lethal weapon. This book is designed in a simple manner, mindful of your busy schedule.

I have tried my best to create it to the best of my ability, only to tear it down twice with my own hands. This third version comes from my heart, and my heart finally said "yes" to its launch.

You will find immense value if you approach it with a curious mind rather than passing judgment on the book and its teachings.

As it's said, "the teacher appears when the student is ready" by Master Choa Kok Sui, founder of modern Pranic Healing. Hence, every word written in this book is energy flowing from my teacher to you through me. You have two choices:

➤ Judge me and my guru's teachings and his wisdom. If you choose choice 1, the judgement that may arise in your mind will be, "this teaching or chapter won't work in my business."

Or

➢ Understand it with a curious mind. And Each time you read anything, ask yourself, "what possibilities can I create to implement this in my business?"

You will choose choice 2 if you are a serious, and growth-hungry developer, and you aspire to achieve your ambitions quickly. Then, this is the only choice.

I wish you all the best and success in the entire universe. Don't overlook the next chapter on how to get 10x value from this book.

The name of my own story is "**Connecting the Dots.**"

I was myself a builder from 2007 to 2012, where I used to develop G+4 high-end luxury apartments in the northern region of Delhi. One day, I got a call from an apartment owner, which I completed five months back in 2012. I went to have a cup of tea with him, and he took me to his room where he showed me a wardrobe that was empty, but when I got closer, it was infested with termites. I was shocked as I had just completed that project five months back. Then, I had two choices at that time:

Choice 1: To say, I have used branded plywood, laminate, and adhesive.

Or

Choice 2: To find a permanent solution.

After doing some study, I discovered that every Indian once in a while needs to deal with the problems of dampness, termite, and borer in their dream home. I therefore took up this big challenge to find a solution. I started with manufacturing door opening and shaft opening solutions using wood polymer composite as a substrate material, which helped real estate builders minimize timelines, budget and maintenance.

I started doing the same. However, the journey from 2013 to 2021 was not easy. I had to deal with all sorts of sales and marketing challenges that come with being an entrepreneur. I tried my hands on several forms of digital marketing and then tried to keep a three-layer team of 30 sales professionals pan-India and many more strategies.

However, still, I was not getting the results I was looking for until I learned the power of leveraging the right marketing before selling and the importance of a deep purpose behind my work, which was just more than me and making money for myself.

The moment I understood that, I was invited to a meeting in January 2023 in Noida with a builder who wanted to replace wooden frames with Duracap 2.0 frames, and they invited me for a presentation. Our meeting was scheduled for Saturday afternoon at 3:15 PM with the group's CEO, who got late.

Meanwhile, I was waiting at the marketing office, and suddenly a customer came in, and I got a chance to overhear the conversation with the sales manager. It didn't align with what a sales conversation should be, and it contradicted the fundamentals taught by my marketing mentor.

Unable to sleep well that night, for the next three days, I visited 19 builders as a mystery buyer, and I noticed something that hit me hard. I observed very hard, pushy sales without building strong authority, trust, and no value addition prior to selling was being done. For them, it was just a transaction, and I was just another person to sell a flat.

Meditating on this problem one fine morning, I made a decision that I wanted to solve a bigger problem for the real estate developers. I delegated the mission of minimizing timelines, budgets, and maintenance for real estate developers to my team and practically told them that I wanted to solve a bigger problem.

That's when I changed my hat from a vendor to a mentor. Initially, I faced a lot of challenges as I approached my existing customers, but they did not give me any importance. It took me a few days to decide that they were looking at me as a vendor.

I did not stop there. I went to a market that was absolutely virgin for us. But, over there, I faced a new challenge. No one trusted me because of the lack of past background awareness.

I solved this problem by meditating again and creating one marketing collateral which had the power to kill every objection in the mind of any builder I wanted to approach. I started with a real estate growth capsule in the form of a magazine named "Build Legacy." This was a game-changer. I sent the magazine's first edition with a letter and got an appointment to speak to him. And the rest is history. It was like the best foot-in-door strategy for me. It was able to create so much urge that so many approached me on LinkedIn and fixed 1-2-1 diagnostic calls with me.

x

Thus, I started with an opportunity to serve over 900 builders to minimize timelines and budgets worth 1000's of crores in 12 years. Then, getting a growth capsule magazine designed for real estate developers named "Build Legacy," creating a deep impact over the fraternity. Finally, serving real estate developers to increase sales velocity by a unique proprietary framework that is creating magic in real estate sales.

Now, when I look back and connect the dots, I recall one line of Steve Jobs:

"You can only connect the dots looking backward and forward."

Now, I realize why everything happened in my life and how God was kind enough to provide the right guidance through the right persons when it was needed at the right time.

This book will certainly benefit every real estate developer, no matter what location, category, or type of development you are involved in. But, as per my experience, being very truthful, you will need my help either to comprehend or implement these concepts or get your team to use the same concept to increase the sales velocity.

Gift: Thus, my bonus gift for you is that I'll be available to you whenever you need assistance understanding or putting these ideas into practice. I will be approachable to you by just booking a 1-2-1 meeting with me. I'm here to help you succeed.

QR Code

Moreover, if you are pretty serious about achieving ambitions fast without wasting your time on hits, trials, and assumptions, then you can also apply for a 1-2-1 diagnostic session with AH. Once you are eligible, I will invite you for an exclusive online masterclass "5 Unknown Sutras of Real Estate Sales."

Since I believe in results, I just take on five companies in a year to transform at a very deeper level, and for that, I would love to work with someone who embodies what I call "Charitrik Gun":

➤ Has high ambitions and wants to accomplish them fast.

➤ Must be aspiring to sell fast at a premium and also be the purple cow of the market and be the number one in the category or location they are operating.

➤ Who does not just want to be dependent on channel partners or signing underwriting mandates to sell the inventory.

➤ Very conductive and receptive to listening.

➤ Must be open for change.

➤ Must be 1st, 2nd, or 3rd generation entrepreneurs either started the real estate developer business himself or his father has started, and he take care of the business.

➤ Free from operational challenges and is ready to implement the new methodology of marketing and sales.

➤ I often get along well with people between the ages of 28 and 45.

➤ Must be experiencing difficulties converting leads into sales, as well as pressure to close deals and manage cash flow.

➤ Must be great at communication.

- ➢ Must be facing some challenges from the marketing team in the context of lead generation.

- ➢ Must not be clear on what is the root cause of all my challenges and would be looking forward to a permanent solution for that.

- ➢ Must be spiritually aligned, at least a bit.

- ➢ Must be hungry for learning, and for him, learning would be as important as earning.

- ➢ Must have attended some training in the past and be open to new learnings.

- ➢ Must be willing to create an impact and serve.

If you can relate to the aforementioned "Charitrik Gun" and want to accomplish goals quickly without squandering time on failures, experiments, and assumptions, don't delay any further and join me.

QR Code

How to Use this Book

The best way to use this book is to apply the following mantras:

1. **Be curious:** Don't be judgmental about the golden teachings shared. Treat them as pure wisdom which you can't buy at any price. Moreover, even if your mind is popping with judgment, just park your judgement in a parking lot and immediately change your question Instead of asking, "It won't work in my business or I don't have time to implement in my business, "ask yourself the right question, "What possibilities can I create to implement the same in bits and pieces?"

2. **Game of viewpoint:** Viewpoint is nothing but the way you look at a situation. Instead of looking from a limited viewpoint, try to see the same situation from an expanded viewpoint.

3. **Law of exhalation and its importance:** Nature is based on the law of giving and taking. In the same way, human breath also works on inhalation and exhalation. When you read anything written in this book, then that is your inhalation.

   Now, imagine for a moment, that you just inhale three deep breaths and you don't exhale, what will happen?

You will feel choked, right? Similarly, there are sections of notes in every chapter and a few questions that are asked. By keeping a pencil in your hand and exhaling what you are feeling will be very important.

Treat this as an implementation live course book.

4. **Be honest to yourself:** Many times, we are not honest with ourselves, and that's why you may get a command in your brain which would be… leave the work… let's just read the book and I will implement after finishing the book.

    Don't do that. Chapter by chapter, just read and exhale, and try to implement. If you face any challenge, follow the next mantra.

5. **Don't assume | Ask and validate | Ask for help:** Instead of giving details in the last chapter, I gave you a gift to speak to me 1-2-1 without any investment. The purpose of being easily approachable is my strong purpose as the intent is to make an impact and transform the trajectory of real estate sales. Thus, ask for help and ask and validate rather than assuming anything in your own head….

6. **Break a big problem into small pieces:** Imagine a big problem as a big paper and divide it into small pieces. If the problem is of conversion, then break it down into conversion at each step and zoom in your focus to solve a smaller problem rather than solving a big problem.

7. **Chew this book:** Don't just read the book; rather, chew each word and chapter again and again. Repetition is the key to deeper clarity.

8. **Be joyful:** Marketing can't be learned and practiced seriously. Thus, being joyful is the key. Moreover, you can learn marketing by being a kid, aka baccha. So, be ready to be as joyous as a kid.

9. **Read in order:** Read in the order and don't skip any page, especially the notes.

Chapter-1

Deep Dive into the Problem

Let's start with a common point: Cash flow is king and is the most important, inevitable metric of the business. Where does this cash originate from?

It originates in the real estate business when inventory gets sold or when cash comes in against the inventory sold. In both cases, inventory has to be sold Thus, sales velocity is the most critical metric which impacts cash inflow in your business.

Less sales velocity is just a symptom and not the cause. Less sales velocity means a lot. What does it mean to you?

Exhalation time

Question 1: Define what less sales velocity means to business?

____

____

____

____

____

____

____

____

____

Question 2: Define what does less sales velocity mean to my sales and other teams?

____

____

____

____

____

____

____

____

Chhod na, likh ke kya karna hai... (Leave it, what's the point of writing it down...)

Question 3: Define how less sales velocity impacts your personal life?

If you have done this work well, you would understand the relevance and criticality of less sales velocity. Let's see as the last step of staircase and visualize what the preceding steps of sales velocity are:

Cash Inflow – Sales Velocity – Sales Conversion – Marketing Visit – Qualified Lead – Enquiry

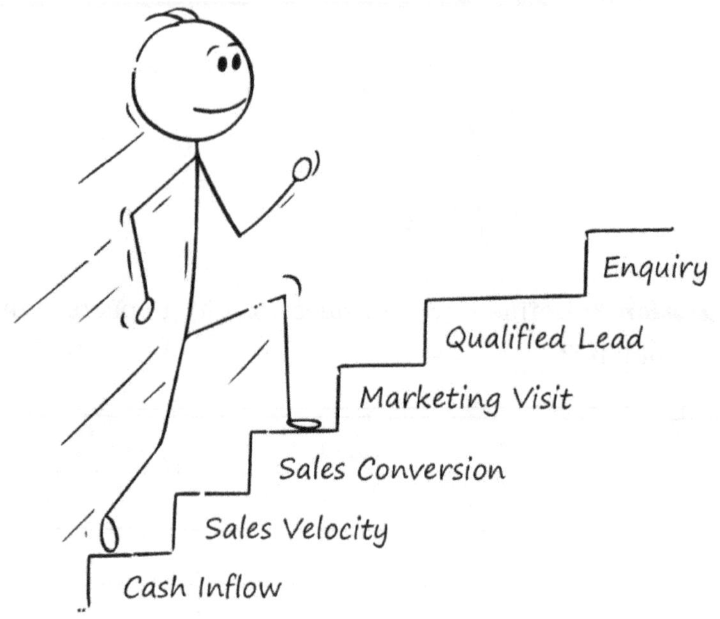

A problem at any step would certainly lead to less sales velocity. Now we know all this, but where to focus to solve this problem from the root...

That is what we are unaware of. My intention is to get you to the root of it.

Before we dive straight into the root cause of the problem, let's understand what are the typical solutions as we try to solve this problem.

Notes:

Chapter-2

Typical Solutions We Do Hit and Trial With

It's said that there are multiple solutions to solve one deep problem.

Exactly, yes. However, most often there arise three situations:

Either we assume a wrong problem as the root cause problem and try to solve that.

Or we try to solve the right problem using a less effective solution because of unawareness.

Or we try to solve the right problem using a less effective solution because everyone is doing it that way, and we assume that it will work for us also, aka we don't challenge and set the new rules.

Now, reflect at the doodle:

Cash Inflow - Sales Velocity - Sales Conversion - Marketing Office Visit - Qualified Lead - Enquiry

Let's start from the bottom of the funnel.

Enquiries

If enquiries are less, what do you do?

Exhalation time

Question 1*:* What typical solutions do I exercise?

____

____

____

____

____

____

____

____

The typical solutions which we practice:

➢ Call a digital agency and ask them to increase the budget or add a new medium digitally, or at the max change some creatives or messaging or change campaigns.

➢ Call an outdoor agency and increase budgets or add a medium or change locations or change creatives or messaging.

➤ Appoint more channel partners or increase their brokerage or, to the max, get into underwriting mandates.

➤ Throw a party to call all channel partners and entertain with an underlying assumption that some booking would come from there or post it.

Qualified Leads

In my recent audits, I have observed that the enquiries to qualified ratio is less, especially in the case of digital medium ads.

If qualified leads are less, what do you do?

Exhalation time

Question 2: What typical solution do I exercise?

____

____

____

____

____

____

____

____

The typical solutions that we practice are:

➤ Again, change campaigns digitally, outdoors, or in print media.

➤ Make some changes in the pitch of the pre-sales team and do some hits and trials on that.

➤ Add or reduce members in the pre-sales team, like adding a quality supervisor to supervise the quality of calls.

➤ Change agency again, being frustrated and assuming that the new agency will be able to solve the problem permanently.

Marketing Office Visits

After speaking to over 400 sales professionals, I have understood a very deep pain point when I ask them what their prospects communicate, which could be the principal reason for fewer site visits.

➤ The customer promises on weekdays that they will be visiting over the weekend, but as Friday comes, they stop taking up calls and don't visit.

➤ They give excuses initially, and then after a point, they stop taking calls.

➤ They judge us and our project, making it difficult to melt their objections at times.

➤ Communication stops after 1 or 2 calls when the client does not show interest.

➢ Customer needs do not match the project inventory: inventory misfit due to location, amenities, size, or many other factors.

➢ The project inventory is out of their budget.

➢ They get a better deal from somewhere else.

If marketing site visits are less, what do you do?

Exhalation time

Question 3: What typical solution do I exercise?

____

____

____

____

____

____

____

____

The typical solutions which we practice:

➢ Create an artificial surge of pricing. Buy now, or else the pricing would increase in the next few days or hours.

➢ Create artificial urgency. Buy now, as there are many people waiting for the same unit.

- ➤ Create some kind of interesting activity for the user to come to the site.

- ➤ Make more frequent calls, send more WhatsApp messages, or retarget more heavily to get them to visit the site. Beg, Borrow, Steal if necessary.

Sales Conversion

Sales conversion of the prospect who visits the site is the ultimate goal of the sales rep. Now, when the sales conversion is less, this is a very painful symptom for any developer.

If sales conversion drops, then what do you do?

Exhalation time

Question 4: What typical solution do I exercise?

____

____

____

____

____

____

____

____

____

The typical solutions which we practice:

➢ Keep reviewing the numbers and see fancy graphs with the whole team and get into analysis paralysis.

➢ Try to make changes either in agency, campaigns, or advertisement medium.

➢ Try to hire some consultants who could help you with increasing the sales conversions.

➢ Try to hire experienced sales professionals who carry great links in the industry to get the instant boost in sales velocity.

Now, let's deep dive into what is the root cause of this problem and then how my sales performance accelerator framework has helped to produce timeless case studies.

Notes:

Chapter-3

The Paradox of Viewpoint

For more than 2 decades of receiving training from the best international mentors, I thought that the job of the teacher or book was to provide good or the best content. However, I could not sleep when I heard this new definition: "The job of the teacher is not to provide some framework or fancy jargon or provide great content, but to expand the student's viewpoint."

This hit me so hard that I realized that this statement could transform my career and the trajectory of how a developer looks at his real estate business. It simplified things for me so much that I can guarantee with my experience that if you are receptive to just learning this principle of expanding your viewpoints, then I can guarantee an increase in your sales velocity in less than 7 days.

I have done this for more than 4 case studies in 2023, selling diverse categories of products in diverse locations.

So, let's dive deep into expanding your viewpoint...

I know you could judge what is the need to understand this theory of viewpoint, or you could think I already know that. My humble request to you is to expand your viewpoint by deleting all judgements coming into your mind to get the most benefit out of it.

Let's understand: What is a viewpoint?

"A way of looking at a situation" (Dekhne ka nazariya)

Your viewpoint is like your stance on things. It's where you position yourself on a topic, your point of view, or how you see something.

"If you always look at things from the same angle, you might miss the bigger picture."

It's also called 'perspective', which comes from the Latin word, "percipere", meaning 'to look through.' Essentially, it's a way of observing or examining something or someone. Perspective is about how you perceive things, your judgment of a situation or fact based on your viewpoint, and the cool part is, you can switch it up whenever you want.

The situation appears to be the same for everyone, but the way you look at the situation makes a different outcome.

Our way of looking at things is shaped by many factors like our upbringing, culture, and experiences. This viewpoint affects how we talk and act. It's important to know that our view might be limited, and this article talks about how sticking to just one way of seeing things can cause problems, using a real story from a competitive industry.

Expanding your Viewpoint

What Do You See?

➢ A Man

➢ A Woman

➢ A Musician Playing a Horn.

➢ A Silhouette

What Do You See?

- ➢ An Old Woman
- ➢ A Young Woman
- ➢ A Woman
- ➢ A Beautiful art

What Do You See?

➢ A Face

➢ A word "LIAR"

What Do You See?

➢ A Tree

➢ A Gorilla

➢ A lion

➢ Two Fish

Expanding your viewpoints:

Expanding your viewpoint in business is a catalyst for innovation, adaptability, and effective decision-making. It brings diverse insights, fosters creativity, and enhances problem-solving, ultimately leading to better outcomes. Understanding various perspectives is key to adapting in a dynamic business environment and successfully meeting customer needs.

➢ **Diverse Insights:** Varied perspectives bring diverse ideas and experiences.

➢ **Innovation:** Exploring different viewpoints fosters creative solutions and opportunities.

➢ **Adaptability:** A broader perspective helps adapt to changing business environments effectively.

➢ **Enhanced Decision-Making:** Considering various viewpoints results in more informed and successful decisions.

➢ **Customer-Centric Approach:** Understanding diverse perspectives aids in tailoring products or services to meet customer needs.

➢ **Effective Problem Solving:** Incorporating multiple viewpoints allows for comprehensive and effective solutions.

➢ **Employee Engagement:** Acknowledging diverse perspectives fosters an inclusive and innovative workplace.

➢ **Market Expansion:** Recognizing and adapting to different market perspectives is crucial for global business success.

Having a single viewpoint is fixed -

FIF- Fixed is Fu..ked

If your viewpoint is fixed, you are likely to get either the same or a worse result.

Remember: If you are Fixed, You are Fu..ked, if you are Flexible, You Grow.

Notes:

____

____

____

____

____

____

____

____

____

____

____

____

____

____

____

____

____

____

Chapter-4

The Million Dollar Viewpoint Shift

The Million Dollar Shift is bringing a shift in your viewpoint. The way you and your team look at sales and marketing are what is very important, which will set the tone for the next few chapters. Your role is not just to adapt but to be proactive in expanding your viewpoint. By doing so, you open yourself to new opportunities and innovative approaches, leading to different and better results.

Limited Viewpoint = Limited Sales

Big Viewpoint = Big Sales = Big Money

Exhalation time

Question 1: How do you look at sales? What is your definition when you hear the word sales?

____

____

____

____

____

____

____

____

____

____

Question 2: How do you listen to the word 'marketing'? What is your definition when you hear this word?

____

____

____

____

____

____

____

____

Question 3: How does your team look at the word 'sales' and how do they define it?

____

____

____

Do this activity with your team and you will notice a lot of similarities to what I am going to share in the next paragraph.

During one of my marketing and sales audits 2.0 conducted at Vera Developers in Mohali, I asked this above question, and the team gave their answers, which I captured on the flip chart.

Real Challenges of 400+ Real Estate Sales Professionals

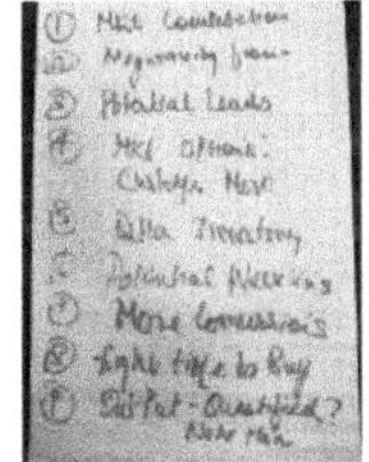 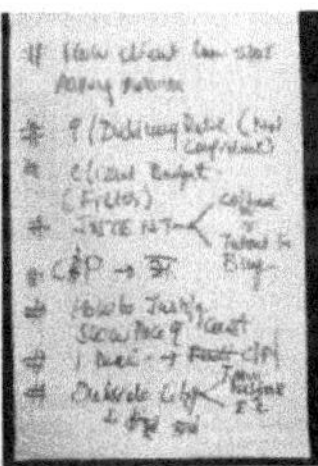 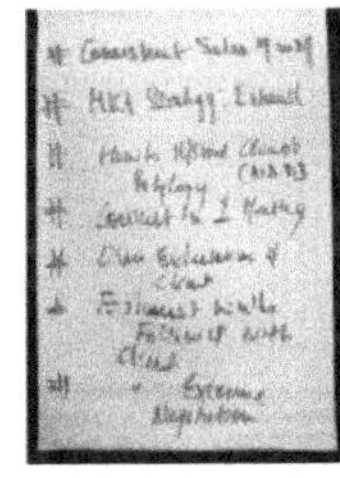 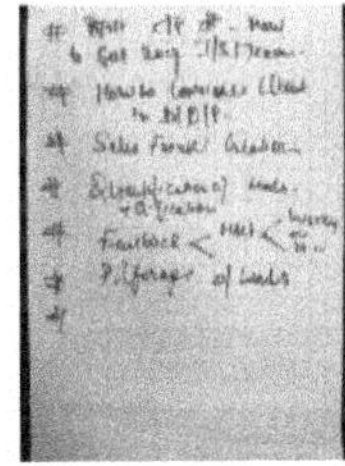

The responses from the sales team were as follows:

➢ Seeing sales as a medium to achieve their targets.

➢ Viewing sales as a means of earning a livelihood.

➢ Considering sales as a way to get incentive.

➢ Selling a product which has unique features matching customer needs.

➢ Interpreting sales as pressure during low times.

➢ Viewing sales as the exchange of product for money, i.e., transaction.

➢ Dealing with customer negotiations and price haggling.

➢ Considering sales as a means to provide someone with their dream home.

➢ Facing 10 rejections to secure one acceptance.

➢ Overcoming objections of customers to secure a positive response.

Similarly, when I asked for the marketing definition from both their team and management, various perspectives emerged:

➢ Marketing is seen primarily as digital marketing.

➢ Advertising projects to create a demand within the target market.

➢ Crafting and delivering the right message using the appropriate medium.

➢ Utilizing marketing as a method to create demand.

➢ Generating the right inquiries through marketing efforts for potential sales.

➢ Using marketing as a tool to ease sales processes.

Now, let me present you with one slide from the '5 Unknown Sutras of Real Estate Marketing' presentation, which will open up new insights and expand your viewpoint.

What Is Selling ?

What Comes in Your Mind When You Hear Word Selling in Your Mind

Exhalation time

Question 1: What difference do you believe there will be at the mindset level if your sales team members operate from a viewpoint of creating trust through education?

____

____

____

____

____

____

____

____

____

The real challenge in your sales velocity lies in team members operating from a viewpoint of selling rather than preparing the prospect to buy. There is a huge distinction between merely selling your product and effectively preparing your prospect to make a purchase. The question arises: "Whose mistake, is it?"

It's not the fault of the sales professional, their leader, or the employer, it's not the mistake of any of them; it's a lack of awareness.

The fact is, "people love to buy but they hate to be sold."

Let's use these two analogies step by step and observe how it works under a microscope from scientific perspective:

Pre sales level at enquiry stage

The fundamental mistake that is often carried out at this stage is that the approach is overly transactional, leading the customer to feel as though they are being sold to, which prompts them to form judgements about the sales representative and the company.

Marketing Site Visit Stage

During the marketing site visit stage, a sales representative is typically trained to ask a set of questions to further confirm the needs identified earlier by the pre-sales team. Following this, there's usually an AV presentation, showcasing of sample flats, presentation of cost sheets, negotiation, and addressing doubts and objections.

However, this entire conversation tends to be highly transactional, and the seller often fails to connect with the prospect and their family on a deeper level. Consequently, after the visit, prospects may avoid picking up calls or make excuses. Furthermore, the flow of the conversation is controlled by the buyer, who interrupts whenever they wish to clarify doubts.

Each sales conversation lacks a standardized structure and tends to be fluid, leading to the Pareto Law principle where only 2 out of 10 sales reps secure 80% of the sales. Consequently, owners often feel very much dependent on these top 2 sales reps.

Even these top performers lack a standardized structure that they can teach to create more replicas of their success, as they too operate from insecurities. This is why real estate companies remain sales-dominated, driven more by sales-oriented individuals rather than sales-driven processes.

Here, "process" refers to standard operating procedures (SOPs), I know that you have 100's of well-defined SOPs, so many that I could make. But I'm referring to something different, which I shall clarify in the upcoming chapter.

Notes:

Chapter-5

The New Definitions of Marketing and Sales

I was asked by my mentor, "What do you mean by Adder?"

I replied, "Someone who adds value!"

He then showcased the next slide, which gave me a shock as 'Adder' meant "A small poisonous snake which has zig zag patterns on its back."

We asked him, "What do you want to teach us with this example?"

He said, "If you don't know the right meaning of a word, how will you make the right sentence out of it?"

That was the day I evolved at every level in my life, when I started looking at every word from a different depth. Do I know it's right meaning or not?

Exhalation time

Question 1: How would you and your team operate if you were to approach selling using this new definition?

____

____

____

____

____

____

____

____

However, the most significant moment came when my mentor introduced us to the power of the right sequence. He gave us an activity to take off our shoes and socks. After we had removed them, he instructed us to put on our shoes first. Once we had done that, he then told us to wear our socks over them.

We were baffled, thinking, "What crazy shit is this?"

But he was trying to teach us a big distinction that we could have never learned any other way!

I learned that anything done correctly but in the wrong sequence can spoil the whole game, whether it's cooking, making a product, or selling a product or a service.

Then he asked me three powerful questions, the answers to which he guided me with just one word:

1. What needs to be done prior to selling to create a buying environment?

2. What needs to be done prior to selling to create an urge in the buyer to buy?

3. What needs to be done to get yeses from the prospects at every step?

The answer was marketing… Then he paused and said, "right marketing."

Now, I know that using the above adder example, you would have an urge to know the right definition of marketing?

This has 4 parts; if we break the definition:

1. Presenting your product, service, idea, or communication

2. To potential customers

3. In such a way

4. As to make them eager to buy

Now, when we talk about marketing, please set aside any thoughts pertaining to advertising, digital marketing, or media buying, as that is just one branch of the whole tree and not the tree itself.

Let me share a classic case study of Alcove Realty here, which will bring the right flavor and deepen your understanding of right marketing.

About Alcove Realty:

One of the most renowned, trusted, and exemplary names in the sphere of real estate, Alcove Realty, spearheaded by the legendary Mr. Amar Nath Shroff, came into existence to set an indelible benchmark with its numerous landmark projects. Alcove Realty was founded by Mr. Amar Nath Shroff – a stalwart and visionary in the Kolkata Real Estate fraternity – who has successfully been in the business of real estate development for many years. With forty glorious years of experience, this '3 Generation' company is beheld with distinction and respect among all the renowned builders in Kolkata, at the helm of the industry.

Let's deep dive into what we discussed in Chapter 3, which was a doodle:

Cash Inflow – Sales Velocity – Sales Conversion – Marketing Visit – Qualified Lead – Enquiry

Enquiry level

What we need to understand here is that after conducting 1-2-1 diagnostic sessions with real estate developers of various categories and locations, what I understood is that they often overlook important aspects of the definition. Let me share how we applied the right marketing definition and achieved results in days, not even weeks!

1. Creative ads are designed focusing solely on the features of the project, just like this:

Now, fundamentally, what you need to understand that:

> "People do not buy products or services, but they buy stories, magic, and relationships"
> *- Seth Godin, Great Marketer -*

When you simply sell your product based solely on its features or benefits, you may think you are differentiating, but in reality, you aren't.

Moreover, features alone are not able to create an urge or eagerness, which is the ultimate job of the marketing.

When the ad creative, whether done digitally or offline, fails to create an urge, that is when we are doing marketing but not the right marketing! Let me share how we doubled the sales velocity in less than 30 days by using the right marketing at every step of the buyer's journey.

We changed the creative from features and benefits to making it value-centric.

We were marketing Ganga Living and we changed it to a value-centric creative, which no one was doing in the market.

It created so much urge in the prospect that the pre-sales team felt so much at ease to get the prospect to the site.

Qualified leads level

At the pre-sales level, a lead is qualified, and previously, their script contained a few questions to qualify the lead, along with sharing project features and benefits, which wasn't creating an urge or eagerness in the prospect. As an outcome of that, the site visit percentage was low, and the pre-sales team felt demotivated when prospects promised to visit the site but did not turn up.

The moment we changed their script, also known as a template, from feature-driven to value-driven, the dynamics of the game completely changed. Earlier, they were pleading for site visits but after disconnecting from their project (product), they began to feel they were in control of the flow.

They started to perceive that they were now doing invitation-based marketing the moment they said, "We have nothing to sell you now. Our intention is that 83% of prospects feel confused in the home buying journey, and they make uninformed decisions, leading to regrets later. Thus, our purpose is to share with you 18 unknown sutras which you must know before buying your dream home.

The biggest learning I induced in the pre-sales team and the entire management was:

"Detach from your product or service and attach to the customer's or prospect's needs and desires."

To truly understand the gravity of this statement, one must put themselves in the shoes of the customer and switch roles from seller to buyer.

Exhalation time

Question 1: You have to consider how you feel when you are being sold to in a pushy way or a non-pushy way, but solely based on features without your secret desires being met. How do you feel?

____

____

____

____

____

____

____

____

____

Story time: Let me share the story of a Bhalu.

A small child was staying in a village near a small jungle. He used to admire Bhalu, (bear) and dreamt that one day he would play with Bhalu.

One fine morning, he was being taught a chapter in which he saw Bhalu, and his desire got triggered. As his school class finished, he went towards the jungle to find Bhalu.

Since his manifestation was strong, he spotted a Bhalu, and he just poked Bhalu, from behind.

The Bhalu, got furious and roared loudly. The child fell behind and injured his elbow. The fearful kid shouted at the peak of his voice.

Listening to it, Bhalu, ran. The kid came back to his home in the evening and went to sleep with his father.

His father was a great marketer, and he asked, "What happened today and how you injured yourself?

The kid told him the whole story, and he said, Beta (son), if you poke the Bhalu, he will roar… So, next, if you want attention and love from Bhalu, then understand first what Bhalu, deeply desires.

The kid said, I don't know that… I haven't asked Bhalu.

His father replied, "Bhalu, loves honey. Thus, do place honey on that path from where the Bhalu, walks every morning and evening. Once the Bhalu, tastes the honey and if he loves it, he will want to meet you again and again."

A simple story can turn your game around…

This is what triggered me when I discovered this challenge. When I first saw a real estate sales professional selling inventory, it gave me a feeling as if he was poking the customer.

This is what I call giving **ECB** to your potential customers: **an Ethical Control Bait:** a bait that triggers and fulfills the secret desires of your Bhalu and gives you a chance to control his behavior.

Bait, What ?

Exhalation time

Question 1: Visualize how your pre-sales team is behaving with your Bhalu? Are they poking your Bhalu (where Bhalu represents your potential customer) at the pre-sales level?

____

____

____

____

____

____

____

____

Marketing Site Visit

Firstly, at this level, you need to become your Bhalu to understand the mind of Bhalu to understand that he comes with a certain set of doubts, confusions, judgments, fears and aspirations too.

You also need to understand deep customer or human psychology in the context of how the human brain works.

Secondly, when a prospect comes for a meeting at the site office, he sits with a lot of judgements which he does not show you… But actually, he is judging the sales rep sitting in front of him on many fronts.

Now, when any person is judging anyone, he is not listening or giving a therapeutic listening to the other person.

Exhalation time

Question 1: Imagine a situation where you are judging anyone, pretending you are listening to him deeply, but, actually, you are not.

____

____

____

____

____

____

Thirdly, when you are saying the same thing which other sales reps said to him when the Bhalu went to other sites, then he feels he also has the same tape. He gets turned off and his judgmental mind activates, and he stops listening and paying attention.

The same challenge we faced at Alcove also at the site visit stage, and that is why we were very clear with one philosophy:

"If competition will zig, we at Alcove will zag."

I mean, as a marketer, your job is to gain the attention of your Bhalu, by creating an urge or eagerness using the same ECB, followed by four phases.

Now, generally, at any site you will go to, the sales rep will start with showcasing you a model post doing need analysis and then show an AV presentation, and then present a cost sheet for finalization.

We broke the flow using the principle which I will showcase to you in a graph. If you understand this, it will change the trajectory of selling in your company.

"People buy people whom they trust and who are first to add massive value."

More example of ECB based ads:

If you give the right ECB to your Bhalu and then add the right value, you are bound to win hearts. However, prior to adding value, you need to understand one principle, that your Bhalu's depth of listening will depend on the level of trust you have won.

1. If your trust is low and you don't add value, your Bhalu will say no or will stop communicating.

2. If your trust is high, but you haven't added any value, Bhalu would say no with a smile.

3. If your trust is low, but value is high, he may say yes, but I still insist on building trust first and then adding value.

4. The top right corner is the slot to be in, which can be achieved if you follow the right sequence: the Bhalu is bound to say yes with a smile, with lots of love and respect.

Always remember: Right marketing can only be done following the right sequence.

Now the question must be popping in your head: how to follow the structure which automatically creates trust in whether anyone opens the conversation and then adds immense value to the Bhalu?

Exhalation time

Question 1: Visualize how your sales team is conducting the selling process. Are they poking your Bhalu (Bhalu referred to as your potential customer) during site visits?

____

____

____

____

____

____

____

____

Yes, you've stumbled upon the right question!

This can only be accomplished through a revolutionary approach to selling, which my mentor taught me, known as the "4-phase structure of selling".

In the 4-phase approach, you're not simply selling; rather, you're preparing your Bhalu, to make a purchase. There is a hell lot of difference in both of them.

It's a psychological, "sequential" selling technique where we don't poke our Bhalu. Instead, it's about 80% of doing right marketing and then 20% of selling. There are three key distinctions here to note and deep dive in:

1. Marketing before selling is the golden key.

2. Right marketing, done correctly, builds trust and sets you apart from the competition.

3. It's about 80% marketing and 20% selling, all in the right sequence.

4 Phase , What is ?

The 4- phase is a BRAND NEW way to selling ......

It is a psychological "sequential " selling technique that is used to prepare People to Buy ...... NOT to Sell.

There are 4 elements of the 4-phase structure, which are as follows in the right sequence:

➢ **Grand Opening:** The agenda of the first phase is to build trust by showcasing authority. The prospect, after seeing this, must feel simply amazed.

➤ **Transformative Content:** The agenda for the second phase is to make the prospect feel that you have added so much valuable content that they did not get from anyone else. The prospect must feel that they have received amazing content. Transformative content is that which clears away all doubts, confusions, and melts all objections in the prospect's mind.

Elements of 4 Phase

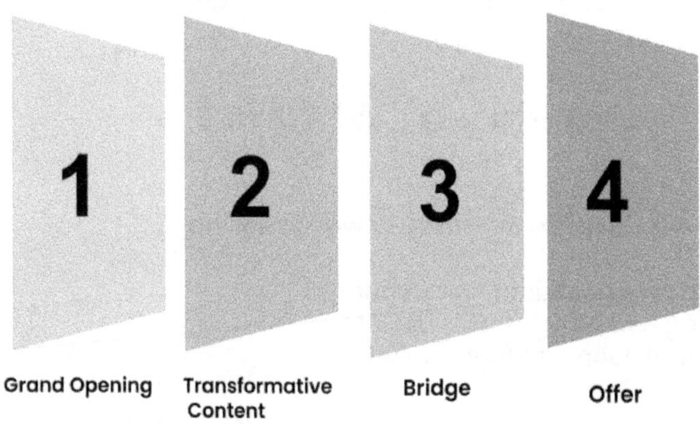

➤ **Bridge:** A bridge is the most critical stage, as obtaining prior consent from the prospect prepares him/her to buy. The actual job of a bridge is to connect from point A to point B. Similarly, in selling, it's important to create a bridge before presenting your product's offer in such a way that it creates eagerness.

➤ **Offer:** The biggest mistake that happens in real estate sales is that we need to understand that your offer has to be equivalent to the amount of trust you have earned. Now, what happens is that you have to sell a 50 lakh or 5 crore flat, but for that, you need to question yourself, "Have I built the trust worth that amount?"

If you have built that level of trust, then it's great. Otherwise, you need to build that trust using strong phases 1 and 2.

If not, you need to give a small offer to your prospect worth 1000 or 2000 rupees. I know this won't land that easily, but we have tried it with multiple developers, and it made the job of sales reps so much easier. Without giving a small offer, they were chasing prospects and kept doing follow-ups with them.

In the case of Alcove, we gave an offer of a home buying assessment protocol and coupled with many other offers that had high perceived value and low cost to the company.

I know that even after seeing proof of concept, your mind may still be judgmental about whether it's really possible.

Yes, if you want to experience the true power of 4 phases, then you can book 1-2-1 diagnostic sessions with AH, and in that, I will tell you where you are stuck in your marketing and sales in less than 15-30 minutes, guaranteed!

Moreover, I would love to give you a free demo of my 4 phase and the 4 phase of multiple builders, which has helped them to print crores fast.

After giving one 4 phase, we qualify them to give a site visit, and then only serious buyers are left.

It eliminates the hide and seek game of follow-up by sales team members. It's pure invitation-based marketing - you invite only those shortlisted prospects who qualify and then give them the 4 phase about your project. This also happens in the 4 phase methodology, followed by apartment showcasing and the offering of irresistible deals, which eliminates negotiation from the picture!

In this whole scenario, from giving the ECB to the first value-driven 4 phase to offering a small incentive to qualify, and then inviting serious project prospects to undergo the next 4 phase, which prepares them to buy, we avoid pushy sales tactics and entering into hard negotiations.

In this whole process, you control the flow and drive the behavior of the prospect.

Notes:

Chapter-6

Let's Deep Dive and Strip Off What's in Your Mind

I still remember when I conducted the marketing and sales audit 2.0; post that, Mr. Yashaswi Shroff, Marketing Director, had a few questions for me. We had a very deep interaction. Similarly, there must be similar doubts or questions running in your mind, which are important to address.

1. **How would all this be implemented?**

    This whole new marketing-dominated, sales-driven approach can be implemented provided you feel you are the right fit (as per Charitrik Gun) mentioned in the earlier chapter. Post that, you need to apply a 1-2-1 diagnostic call with AH, in which I will get you to the root of the low sales velocity and after that, I will be showcasing you 5 unknown sutras in real estate sales. After that, if you qualify on certain parameters, we begin with real mentoring and implementation.

2. **Why would I personally need to be involved and how much time would I need to invest?**

    As mentioned earlier, with this new approach, you need to drive the change and set new benchmarks for your team. Then you become the navigator for your team. This is the only function of doing right marketing, which you must do for 6-8 hours every day for 60 days. Post that, your results will get you in love so much that you will just do this.

3. **Can't my team directly learn and use the 4-phase methodology?**

In one word, "no."

4. **Will my existing team be able to use the 4-phase methodology, or would I need a new team for the same?**

Yes, your existing team will be able to learn, but first, you or anyone from senior management must lead the change and then teach the same team.

5. **Will the same system work for any category or location?**

Yes, the science is based on human psychology and the fundamentals of right marketing. I have tested it in small and big markets and also in residential and commercial categories of projects.

6. **Would I need to invest some resources or financial resources to implement the 4-phase methodology?**

You don't need to add any additional budget for marketing or advertising. You just need to invest your time and energy in unleashing the hidden marketer in you.

7. **How would it increase my cash flow by increasing sales velocity and reducing interest costs? How much time would it take to start producing results?**

Certainly, yes, it will boost cash flow in less than 30 days once we implement it correctly with complete intensity. Even if we increase sales velocity by 1.5 times, you can imagine the months and interest saved. It takes less than 30 days to implement phase 1 of mentoring and produce results.

8. **What if I am dependent on channel partners (CPs)? Will it still help me increase my sales velocity?**

   Even when the customer comes through CPs, the project presentation is given by the sales team of the builder, and you also need to implement the right marketing before selling. Once done correctly, it will produce results and increase sales velocity.

9. **If someone has no in-house sales team, will your model help to increase sales of our CP?**

   Yes, in that case, the enrollment and mentoring have to be done by the owner of CP.

10. **How will you address it if my team shows resistance to implement something new?**

    Once the owner starts increasing sales velocity and the team sees the results, they also buy results. In fact, after phase 1 of mentoring is implemented, I have observed that the sales team gets eager to learn. It's just that a few of them who will be receptive to change will develop eagerness firstly to learn, and a few would develop later.

11. How will the 4-phase system help reduce marketing cost?

Once you understand, practice, and master right marketing, you will be able to make decisions much faster that will produce the fastest ROI at least expense. Certainly, you can expect a 40% or more reduction in marketing costs.

❖   ❖   ❖   ❖

Notes:

Chapter-7

The Alcove Story: Real Results and Its Roadmap

Let me share the real results, but before that, let me share with you the roadmap we followed to achieve these results.

In the first month only, we were able to increase the sales velocity. In fact, we were able to accomplish last month's unit sales in just 18 days.

Step 1: *Lead marketing yourself and don't delegate it until you master right marketing:*

The transformation we brought about was that I chose Yashaswi Shroff to lead marketing and to drive this whole change; he was primarily responsible on the ground.

The biggest mistake developers make in getting any change, specifically in marketing and sales, is that they hire a consultant and delegate the responsibility to a team member to drive the change and take the onus of it.

This change can be more effectively driven by the developer himself, testing himself, setting new benchmarks, and then slowly delegating it after you have mastered the science yourself.

The first step lays down the foundation for long-term success.

Step 2: *Laser-sharp focus on doing the right marketing and building a marketing - dominated, sales - driven organization:*

On the first day when I saw the calendar of Yashaswi Shroff, I could tell that he was involved in purchasing, sales, and marketing meetings.

There was zero time spent with the customer. I met his father and took his consent to take over all purchase activities for the next 90 days. Moreover, I took the consent from his sister to handle all operational matters and meetings with agencies related to marketing and sales. Yashaswi's laser focus was solely on speaking to existing customers and interacting with them for a specific agenda.

Then, his next agenda was to give the 4 phase to customers and make the sales team learn the new science. The whole agenda is to make a marketing-dominated, sales-driven organization.

Step 3: *Be approachable to existing customers:*

The biggest mistake builders make is that as their scale increases, their distance from their customers or prospects also increases. I eliminated these distances, as no one from management was in touch with the prospects or customers. I made it very clear from day 1 to be approachable to customers and prospects (without the fear of whether they call me back or approach me for small matters).

Step 4: *Know your customers well and their secret desires:*

Being approachable to existing customers and prospects gave us access to their secret desires, pain points, and objections which stop them from buying. This further helped us to incorporate them into our 4 phase offering, which increased the conversion effortlessly.

Step 5: *Transformed positioning and business card:*

Instead of positioning ourselves as just another real estate developer, we changed our positioning to "home buying scientists."

We designed a new business card that looked like this:

Business card

Step 6: *Transforming LinkedIn profile, positioning, and constant value to simplify home buying science:*

Yashaswi Shroff had a dormant account on LinkedIn. We took over the account and did complete profile optimization and positioned him as a home buying scientist. Most buyers checked his profile, which helped build better trust. We also started posting valuable posts on LinkedIn to educate and simplify the home buying process.

Step 7: *Creating ECB, 4-phase, and initiating 1-2-1 4-phase sessions, producing results:*

As shown earlier, we prepared ECB, which was able to create enough urge and eagerness in the prospect to listen. It allowed us to control the flow. The first value 4 phase, consisting of 18 unknown sutras, was able to create 10x trust and value. This helped to filter out serious prospects and increase conversion.

Step 8: *Created another 4-phase project for ultra-serious prospects and prepared them to buy:*

Creating another project-based 4 phase for serious prospects helped showcase and distinctively position the project, creating an urge in the prospects.

Step 9: *Activated the data of over 50,000 active prospects and sent them value-driven baits:*

Out of the existing database, which was maintained and had 1.7 lakhs who enquired in the past, stored on Salesforce, we filtered based on certain criteria and identified approximately 50k prospects. We started keeping in touch and establishing connections with them using the right marketing approach.

Step 10: *Future steps in the pipeline:*

There are many future steps in the pipeline which we will implement and share its results in the next edition of the book.

Now, you must be thinking about the results produced by implementing the above roadmap. The results were phenomenal and are mentioned below:

Results

➤ Marketing is sales driven, and not sales dominated.

➤ Increase in sales velocity.

- Overall project sales by December 2024 instead of the earlier planned December 2025.

- Huge saving of interest costs from one-year prior sales.

- Acquisition of the next very big land parcel and starting to build one of the largest projects in Kolkata.

- Positioning as home buying scientists.

- 10x authority by launching a book "18 Sutras You Must Know Before Buying Your Dream Home."

- 3x referrals with super ease.

- 50% reduction in ad budgets in the next 90 days will be done, and results will be more.

- 50% reduction in retainership of agencies who were working as it was not required.

- Reduction in team members who were non-productive and not ready for change.

- 10x deep connection between customers and owners.

- Implementation of 1-2-many format of selling and selling directly at director level to 30-40 prospects at one time.

- Much fewer follow-ups by pre-sales and sales team: either it gets to yes or no.

- Standardized structure for marketing and selling without any dependency on a person.

- Zero fear of any sales or marketing professional leaving.

➤ Better attrition because the team also loves to be around a leader who acts as a torchbearer.

➤ Zero fear of how your team will pitch the property as you as a business owner do.

➤ Hassle-free training of your sales team.

➤ Massive reduction in roadside advertising.

Notes:

Chapter-8

The 2 Choices

By this chapter, you must be thinking, "Ankur, why have you shared everything so transparently?" One of my mentors guided me to "share the most secret stuff for free."

So, what have I done? I have shared all that I have learned out of 100's of meetings, several audits, and a handful of mentoring assignments I am working on.

Now you have 2 choices:

1st choice

I have told you everything, and you can implement it yourself. However, as per my experience, you would face a lot of hurdles, and the cost you would pay for that would be huge.

Else, you can move ahead with the 2nd choice:

2nd choice:

You can have me and my team by your side and implement with ease, and experience sales and profit growth in less than 30 days (without zero stress and no hits and trials).

If you wish to go ahead with the 2nd choice, then certainly, I have a super irresistible offer mentioned in the last chapter for you.

Chapter-9

The Smart Choice

Thanks for making the smart choice by choosing the 2nd choice.

If you are a serious, growth-hungry developer, then I have a super exciting offer for you.

Offer #1:

1-2-1 diagnostic session with AH.

Offer #2:

1-year subscription of Growth Capsule Magazine.

Offer #3:

Value nuggets on LinkedIn